Anaconda/ Anaconda

By Johanna Burke   Traducción al español: Eduardo Alamán

 **Gareth Stevens**
Publishing

Please visit our Web site, www.garethstevens.com. For a free color catalog of all our high-quality books, call toll free 1-800-542-2595 or fax 1-877-542-2596.

Cataloging Data

Burke, Johanna.
Anaconda/Anaconda / Johanna Burke.
    p. cm. — (Killer snakes / Serpientes asesinas)
Includes bibliographical references and index.
ISBN 978-1-4339-4527-4 (library binding)
1. Anaconda—Juvenile literature. I. Title.
QL666.O63B87 2011
597.96'7—dc22

2010024028

First Edition

Published in 2011 by
Gareth Stevens Publishing
111 East 14th Street, Suite 349
New York, NY 10003

Copyright © 2011 Gareth Stevens Publishing

Designer: Michael J. Flynn
Editor: Greg Roza
Spanish translation: Eduardo Alamán

Photo credits: Cover, pp. 1, (2–4, 6, 8–10, 12, 14–16, 18, 20–24 snake skin texture), 21 Shutterstock.com; p. 5 (green anaconda) Brian Kenny/Taxi/Getty Images; p. 5 (yellow anaconda) Mike Powles/Photolibrary/Getty Images; p. 7 Mary Ann McDonald/Visuals Unlimited/Getty Images; p. 9 Ishara S. Kodikara/AFP/Getty Images; p. 11 Partridge Prod. Ltd./Photolibrary/Getty Images; pp. 13, 15 Ed George/National Geographic/Getty Images; p. 17 iStockphoto.com; p. 19 Tom Brakefield/Stockbyte/Getty Images.

Printed in the United States of America

CPSIA compliance information: Batch #CW11GS: For further information contact Gareth Stevens, New York, New York at 1-800-542-2595.

Contents

- -

Contenido

Boldface words appear in the glossary/
Las palabras en **negrita** aparecen en el glosario

Giant Snakes

Anacondas belong to the boa family of snakes. There are four kinds of anacondas. Green and yellow anacondas are the most common. The green anaconda is the largest kind. It is one of the biggest snakes in the world!

Serpientes gigantes

Las anacondas pertenecen a la familia de las boas. Hay cuatro clases de anacondas. Las más comunes son las anacondas verdes y amarillas. La anaconda verde es la más grande en su clase. ¡Es una de las serpientes más grandes del mundo!

green anaconda/
anaconda verde

yollow anaconda/
anaconda amarilla

5

Anacondas live in South America. Most live in the Amazon **rain forest**. Anacondas like hot, wet places. They are sometimes called water boas because they are very good swimmers. They also climb trees.

- -

Las anacondas viven en América del Sur. La mayoría vive en la **selva tropical** de Amazonas. A las anacondas les gusta el clima caliente y húmedo. En ocasiones se les llama boas acuáticas por su gran habilidad para nadar. Además trepan en los árboles.

7

Baby Snakes

A female anaconda can have between 20 and 50 babies at one time—sometimes more! A baby green anaconda is about 2 feet (60 cm) long. The mother does not care for the babies after they are born. They can hunt and swim right away.

Anacondas bebé

Las anacondas hembra pueden tener entre 20 y 50 bebés a la vez, e incluso más. Las anacondas recién nacidas miden unos 2 pies (60 cm) de largo. Las mamás no cuidan a los bebés después de nacidos. Las anacondas bebé pueden cazar y nadar desde que nacen.

Lunchtime!

A hunting anaconda hides in water and waits for an animal to come by. It quickly bites the animal. Then it wraps its long body around the animal. Like all boas, it kills the animal by **squeezing** it. Then the anaconda swallows the animal whole!

- -

¡A comer!

Las anacondas se esconden en el agua en espera de su presa. De pronto, muerden y se enroscan en el cuerpo de su víctima. Las anacondas matan a sus presas con un **apretón**. ¡Luego se las tragan completas!

11

The Green Anaconda

The green anaconda is sometimes called the giant anaconda because it is so huge. It can grow to 30 feet (9 m) long and weigh more than 550 pounds (250 kg)! Females are much larger than males.

La anaconda verde

A la anaconda verde se le llama anaconda gigante. ¡Puede medir hasta 30 pies (9 m) de largo y pesar más de 550 libras (250 kg)! Las hembras son mucho más grandes que los machos.

13

Green anacondas eat deer, fish, **caimans**, birds, and turtles. They often hide in water and **attack** animals that come to drink. After a green anaconda kills an animal, it drags the meal into the water.

Las anacondas verdes comen venados, peces, **caimanes**, aves y tortugas. Con frecuencia se esconden en el agua y **atacan** a los animales que se acercan a beber. Tras atrapar a su víctima, la anaconda la arrastra al agua.

The Yellow Anaconda

The yellow anaconda is much smaller than the green anaconda. However, it is still big. Yellow anacondas can be more than 12 feet (3.7 m) long. They can weigh more than 40 pounds (18 kg). Females are larger than males.

La anaconda amarilla

La anaconda amarilla es mucho más pequeña que la verde. Pero aun así es muy grande. Las anacondas amarillas pueden medir más de 12 pies (3.7 m) de largo. Además pueden pesar más de 40 libras (18 kg). Las hembras son más grandes que los machos.

17

Yellow anacondas eat birds, **rodents**, fish, turtles, and young caimans. Just like green anacondas, they like to hunt from the water. However, yellow anacondas may also hunt on land.

Las anacondas amarillas comen aves, **roedores**, peces, tortugas y caimanes jóvenes. Tal y como lo hacen las anacondas verdes, las amarillas cazan desde el agua. Pero las anacondas amarillas también cazan en la tierra.

People and Anacondas

There are many reports about anacondas attacking people. However, these might just be stories. Anacondas don't usually attack people. Most anacondas will allow people to touch them and even pick them up. Some people keep them as pets!

La gente y las anacondas

Existen muchos reportes de ataques de anacondas. Sin embargo, estos pueden no ser ciertos. Las anacondas no suelen atacar a las personas. La mayoría de las anacondas incluso se dejan tocar por las personas. ¡Muchas personas las usan como mascotas!

Snake Facts/
Hoja informativa

Green Anaconda/
Anaconda verde

Length/Longitud	20 to 25 feet (6 to 7.6 m); up to 30 feet (9 m) De 20 a 25 pies (6 u 7.6 m) hasta 30 pies (9 m)
Weight/Peso	400 to 500 pounds (180 to 230 kg); up to 550 pounds (250 kg) De 400 a 500 libras (180 a 230 kg) hasta 550 libras (250 kg)
Where It Lives/ Hábitat	hot, wet rain forests in South America Selvas tropicales en América del Sur
Life Span/ Años de vida	10 to 30 years in the wild de 10 a 30 años en libertad
Killer Fact/ Datos mortales	If the meal is big enough, an anaconda can go without eating again for months. Some have even gone years without eating! Si su comida es bastante, la anaconda puede pasar sin comer durante meses. ¡Algunas han pasado años sin comer!

Glossary/Glosario

attack: to try to harm someone or something

caiman: a type of small alligator

rain forest: a forest that gets lots of rain

rodent: a small, furry animal with large front teeth, such as a mouse

squeeze: to press something tightly

- -

apretón (el) apretar algo muy fuerte

atacar tratar de dañar a algo o alguien

caimán (el) un lagarto pequeño

roedores (los) pequeños animales peludos con largos dientes, como los ratones

selva tropical (la) una selva en la que llueve mucho

For More Information/Más información

Books/Libros

Ganeri, Anita. *Anaconda*. Chicago, IL: Heinemann Library, 2011.

Smith, Molly. *Green Anaconda: The World's Heaviest Snake*. New York, NY: Bearport Publishing, 2007.

Web Sites/Páginas en Internet

Anaconda

www.kidzone.ws/lw/snakes/facts-anaconda.htm
Read about anacondas and other killer snakes.

Anacondas

kids.nationalgeographic.com/kids/animals/creaturefeature/ anaconda
Read about anacondas and see a video of one in action.

Index/Índice